THE PIANO MUSIC OF
Joseph Haydn
Eleven favourite pieces

Kevin
Mayhew

We hope you enjoy *The Piano Music of Joseph Haydn.*
Further copies are available from your local music shop.

In case of difficulty, please contact the publisher direct:

The Sales Department
KEVIN MAYHEW LTD
Rattlesden
Bury St Edmunds
Suffolk IP30 0SZ

Phone 01449 737978
Fax 01449 737834

Please ask for our complete catalogue of outstanding Instrumental Music.

Front Cover: *The Five Senses: The Sense of Hearing* by Philippe Mercier (1689-1760).
Courtesy of Roy Miles Gallery/The Bridgeman Art Library, London.
Reproduced by kind permission.
Cover designed by Graham Johnstone and Stephen Judd.

Ths compilation first published in Great Britain in 1996 by Kevin Mayhew Ltd.

ISBN 0 86209 911 0
Catalogue No: 3611218

0 1 2 3 4 5 6 7 8 9

Printed and bound in Great Britain

Contents

ALLEGRO MODERATO from SONATA IN G

Joseph Haydn (1732-1809)

MINUET AND TRIO IN A

Joseph Haydn

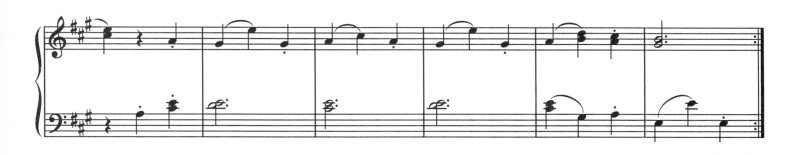

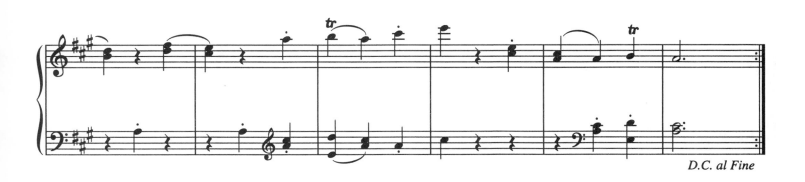

D.C. al Fine

GERMAN DANCE

Joseph Haydn

Fine

D.C. al Fine

MINUET IN C MINOR

Joseph Haydn

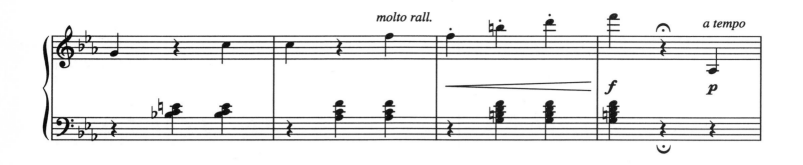

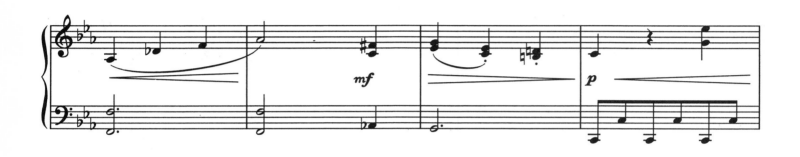

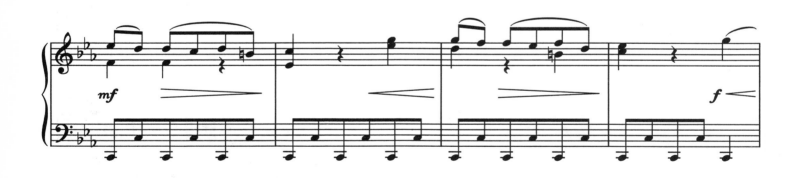

ANDANTE from SONATA IN G

Joseph Haydn

ALLEGRO from SONATA IN C

Joseph Haydn

MINUET IN C

Joseph Haydn

D.C. al Fine

MINUET AND TRIO IN B♭

Joseph Haydn

Fine

D.C. al Fine

FINALE from SONATA NO 24

Joseph Haydn

MINUET AND TRIO from SONATA NO 15

Joseph Haydn

Fine

D.C. al Fine

TRIO from SONATINA

Joseph Haydn